CIGAR CHRONI
OF THE LEAF P
STORYTELLING

by

Keya S. McClain

KEYA S. MCCLAIN

ISBN: 978-1-7356157-0-7

Book Cover Design by: *Rose Miller with creative assistance from Jeff Davis (Astute)*
Photo Credit: *Gregory Jones ig: saintgregorycreates*
Branding & Stylist: *Tamara Batsell ig: tbstyleworks*
Cigar Lounge photographed: *The Boardroom Whisky and Cigar Lounge* (Fort Worth, Texas)
www.theboardroomdfw.com

Settle in and read about the cigar experience, lifestyle and culture from my perspective. You may find some similarities, differences or thoughts that shape your own experience or cause intrigue for you to explore. Keya S. McClain

My introduction to cigars was an evening invite that changed my socialization and lifestyle experience. Cigars is a comradery connection. Women weren't smoking cigars the way I see now and I am glad that it has evolved for women cigar smokers. Although I still wouldn't consider myself a cigar connoisseur by any means - I definitely enjoy the soothing and relaxing vibe it provides. I enjoy walking in a cigar lounge and nestling in a corner and smoke and reflect or smoke and spark up a conversation with complete strangers. The influence of a smoke and drink mixed with great conversation provides a comfort similar to comfort food. A comfort only a cigar can provide. An indulgence that is simplified to putting smoke in the air. Cigars that are filled with tobacco and a leaf with various taste that add to the experience. My desire to indulge almost daily stems from my palette requirement and need for an end of the day relaxation or morning retreat. I am clearly a lover of the leaf still learning and finding value in recommendations and suggestions. The connections are breathtaking and refreshing. I have shared my experiences and the value cigars provide in my life in poetic form. Merging my life's pleasures for all to enjoy.

DEDICATION & ACKNOWLEDGEMENTS

I would like to thank each and every person that supports, acknowledges and appreciates my work. To those that read parts of the book and provided feedback and personal reviews. To those in Smokin Haute who support my weekly poetry live reading and to Ayokie who supports my work in her group "Smokin Haute." The vision was bought to life with photographer Greg and branding and stylist sister Tamara. This book is dedicated to all of my fellow brothers and sisters of the leaf (BOTL & SOTL). I extend my appreciation to the various cigar lounges that have welcomed me and supported my work, my presence and cigar requests. My hope is that you enjoy and capture great moments as you put some smoke in the air! Keep it Smokey!

Keya

Smoking Reading Contents

WHAT'S YOUR STRONGEST DESIRE

To ignite the fire.

Produce the highest flame.

From the first hit of the stogie.

The cigar has climaxed and came.

Bursting with flavor.

Your palate just enjoys and savors.

The aroma and taste is robust.

And you may trust.

That on the very first thrust.

This smoke is especially for you.

I can tell that you are going to last.

You won't be a quickie or give up too fast.

You burn slow.

It's the route we're taking.

Best believe this ain't no fakin.

I'm happy about the way things are developing.

Never second guessed and definitely not settling.

On any gentleman.

Or the selection of cigars.

This sister of the leaf has bars.

And if you smoke with her under the stars.

You'll be the happiest and luckiest of all the cigars.

EACH TIME

Each time I can smoke.

The tension and stress is released.

The creases in my cheek slowly decrease.

And I find myself completely relaxed.

A drink or two as I blow on a few.

Keeping smoke in the air.

Leaned back in my chair.

Ready to just get there.

Peaceful and quiet time alone.

Reflecting on what is next.

Taking steps to ensure it is my very best.

By the end of the night I feel refreshed.

I've smoked a few.

Now sitting back.

Grateful there is no lack.

Many times, to stay on track

I'm tracking my sticks.

When is the next order being delivered?

And I start to consider.

Why not order some more?
Let's see what CI has in store.
Or maybe I'll get that bid.
And get excited like a kid.

I DON'T KNOW

I don't know what else to say.

You typically make my day

Your aroma is around to stay.

I found refuge in the relaxation that you provide.

Thank you for being along for the ride.

The smoke in the air is making it clear.

You are my dear.

Stogies and coffee in the morning crisp air

To whisky and sticks

Licking the tip

And getting you right.

The flame from the torch will make you boast.

The various gages and aroma you provide.

I enjoy you from beginning to end.

The greatest prize.

At the end, I've had the best surprise

And my poker comes out to get that last smoke.

IN MY BOX

In my box, I've lined you up.

After a good re-up.

My humidor is looking good.

I'm ready to chill and smoke.

Kick my feet up and blow.

I'm on my way to relax.

Not as good as my highest climax.

But, I'm sure to feel the chill.

Although I had a bout and was ill.

It left me to reflect.

Be more real and direct.

And enjoy the best feeling of peace.

You can't encounter it without the inner release.

As I smoke and go within.

I find myself digging deep in.

Revealing some sin.

Released with a pen.

RATHER UNIQUE

It's rather unique.

And quite distinct.

The way the stick is rolled.

Easy to maintain and control.

You must maintain the proper temperature.

You don't want too much moisture.

Set your drink on the coasters.

And have a great time with the enthusiast in the room.

No need to assume.

Just make it soon.

Grab yourself a Dallas Leaf Cigar.

And don't go too far.

You'll be back to purchase more.

That stick will make you adore.

No one has to encourage or implore.

You will want the greatest stick in the humidor.

Won't have you pocket poor.

If you disagree do your research and compare.

It's a smooth smoke.

Won't make you choke.

But, the emotions evoked.

Won't make you laugh

Because it's no joke.

The 1841 DL will have you wanting more.

It's great to explore smoking it down to the tip.

KEYA S. MCCLAIN

CLOSURE OF THE DAY

This is my closure of the day.

Awakening of a new day.

I woke up with no intentions to play.

I chose my stick of choice.

Decided to use my voice.

Short of what I've been blessed and chosen to do.

I can't be concerned and caught up in you too.

Taking this time to reflect.

Sometimes you must be direct.

I will always protect…

My name.

And expect you to do the same.

From the moment I came.

Shining light in the dark space.

And we can certainly dress it up in lace.

Light that fire.

Oh yea, go figure.

What a nice way to chill and relax.

By the time you decrease in size.

I taste a distinct surprise.

8

You leave me wanting more.

Going back in the darkness to explore.

You are a great way to escape.

Sometimes, when I lay awake.

I can retreat to you.

No matter the season.

I always find a reason.

To light you up.

We continue to fight COVID

You know it!

LOVE THE WAY YOU FEEL

I love the way you feel.

Long and fat.

You fit perfectly in my hand.

You don't mind that I spin you around.

Only to get you to burn evenly in my mouth.

I release your ash.

After I've sucked for so long you just can't last.

By the end of our time.

I'm feeling fine.

That deep and tasty stick has said it's goodbye.

LICK YOUR TIP

I lick your tip to get you wet.

Then I light you up and you start to sweat.

I suck all the way down to the bottom of your stick.

Stroking you periodically to show my love.

You are my true, devoted and loyal brown man.

I'm not picky about the hues of your brown.

All I know is you never make me frown.

Keeps me satisfied and happy until the last drag.

My associate comes by and drops off a bag.

Full of cigar treats.

This can't be beat.

This will definitely be the tip that lasts.

THANK YOU

How can I thank you?

Can't show my appreciation enough.

At first, it started off rough.

I wasn't fully aware that my first inhale would cause me to

choke.

Reached down to the pit of my throat.

But, I was coached.

Helped to find the flavors and blends.

So I transcended higher.

Understanding the way to hold you in my hand.

To when to remove the band.

The breaks in between the drags.

And that the cost wasn't the only way to brag.

I'm thankful for the various times you've kept me company

in my lowest and brightest of times.

Your loyalty has been unmatched.

I can have you with dinner or a snack.

So many assume things about you.

Most of what they think isn't true.

I realized the way you can change my day.

From stressful to relaxed.

YOU SHOWED UP

You showed up and I knew you would.

If I could I would list it all out.

Your every positive attribute.

The way you relax me from my body to mind.

No confusion.

No chaos.

Just peace.

Not giving me a piece of you.

You have given me all of you.

I get to take the full aroma in.

If I'm smoking you outside.

I can pull in the wind.

Discovery you was the best.

When put to the test.

Any doubts were put to rest.

I became so relaxed with you.

Settling in comfortably and smoking you from beginning to end.

We don't have to pretend.

No need to compromise and bend.

You full extend.

Lighting you up gives me so much pleasure.

You are the real treasure.

The best part…

Well, let's go, just start!

UNCERTAIN TIMES

In the most uncertain of times.

While we are confined.

We should lean on our faith and strength to continue to push through.

Keep smoking, keep raising a glass.

We will definitely last.

Soon, this situation will be a thing of the past.

But, in the meantime have a beer on draft.

Just pour it in your personal glass.

Make that whiskey neat.

Your best cigar is a treat.

Make your day and week complete.

So light up that heat and smoke your best stick.

And as we retreat.

Keep it discrete.

FEET PROPPED UP

Feet propped up.

With my cropped top.

Smacking my lips together because my gloss is popping.

And there's no stopping

This sister of the leaf

She deserves all the treats.

From a stick that's infused to battered and a little abused.

The humidor held you just right.

That wrapper is tight.

I may have to bust you loose.

And there's ultimately no excuse.

For not indulging in you.

See…I've chosen a few.

But, you make it all complete.

And although some may try to compete.

You have them all beat.

The smoke that engulfs around me.

The feeling of relaxation and satisfaction.

And to take you away would be worse than an abstraction.

You are my greatest distraction.

The one that makes sure I disconnect

To reconnect.

Disengage to reengage.

And no matter the gage

Of my smoke

This lifestyle is no joke.

In fact, I'm stoked.

Ready to explore more of you.

Committed and dedicated to what we have.

The relationship is not bad.

As time goes by, our relationship grows.

Yes, you may propose.

This is lifetime goals.

My stogie and I.

WHEN WE STARTED

When we started

Lips departed.

Convinced that we were on to a great start.

Your flavor is just what I imagined.

You'll go down as one of the greatest legends.

Knowing that I was engulfed in your smoke.

I held back nothing.

Licking my top lip to taste that flavor once more.

The way you made me embrace you between my fingers.

To the way you had me feel with a great drink on chill.

Most are surprised by my thrill.

Captivated at how I twirl you in my mouth.

Ensuring you burn evenly and doing all that I can to enjoy
you to the fullest.

You are my greatest night cap.

My morning motivation.

The mid-day shift that will boost me up.

I trust that your flavor won't be too robust.

But, you may just make me bust.

Bust out my humidor and search for more.

Let's see what you have in store.

See, you've spoiled me.

I can't do anything else because you'll turn hard on me.

I won't get you back.

So, I'll sit back and relax with you.

All of you.

Whether you extend all the way for me or prefer to be a
nub.

I'm here for you.

Just as you are here for me.

Been here through various life circumstances.

Divorce, death and life.

Celebrations and just congregating.

I applaud you for being my right hand stick.

You continue to get me through.

GREAT SMOKE

The ability to take something natural and turn it into a great smoke.

No inhaling though, or you'll choke.

The roll and wrapper produces the stogie.

How can you be so certain that this relationship would be over?

This is long term for me.

This is one relationship I won't leave.

The one that makes me feel relaxed and esteemed.

It's the culture.

The way the stick is sculpted.

I have my eyes on you.

A great surprise you are.

Each puff is more relaxing than the previous one.

You know exactly how to fulfill my relaxing desire.

I won't perspire.

Will continue to admire.

You are a work of art.

Making my senses go off the chart.

Come smoke with me.

Releasing smoke in the air.

I know that life isn't always fair.

You must make the best of it and try to repair.

The varying things in life that are thrown our way.

Your strength and tenacity will be on full display.

Get you a stick, sit back and relax and let the smoke do its thing in the air.

SENSES ARE HEIGHTENED

My senses are heightened.

The humidor is equipped with more lighting.

I'm eager to explore and see which cigar I will light.

It's time to take flight.

And once we land we'll be able to take our stick and ignite.

The flames that create a cloud of smoke.

The best type of smoke ain't no joke.

Will leave you revoking most.

If you get too close.

You'll become comatose.

Ready to sit back and relax.

Go into a deep slumber once the day is complete.

Feeling satisfied that you granted yourself a treat.

Having a good smoke is so sweet.

It releases the stresses and strain of the day.

You can have it your way.

Pick any cigar you'd like on display.

Save your bands.

If they stand a chance.

Protect them from the heat.

You can create a personal treat.

SMOKE

The way I took it in.

You can't pretend.

This was bound to happen from the beginning.

Our connection from the flame you put out.

To the relaxation that came about.

I'm into you.

Comfortable and appreciative to the peace you bring.

It's not a fling.

And quite honestly you are one of my favorite things.

A great past time.

But, I also get in a zone with you and it's showtime.

As I spit poetic words refined.

And now you can unwind.

With words and a cloud of smoke.

You feel like you are off on a trip and remote.

I'll be the keynote.

As you blow smoke.

The other refined moment you have as you relax.

Sit back.

I'll make it clear.

That I'm the one you want to hear.

Magic to your ears.

As you indulge in the relaxation of a great stogie.

You'll feel carefree.

But, she's not free.

The stogie ain't either.

It takes investment in this pleasure.

So, I'll see you at the next show.

RATHER AMAZING

The way you are when I smoke is rather amazing.

I'm compelled to tell you that there is no other like you.

I can't concentrate on anything else but getting to choose.

Watching the clock so I can get to you at the end of my

day.

You make it all go away.

The first puff

And things have moved fast.

You're the one that'll last.

When all else fails

I'm devoted to you.

Which stick should I get.

The aromas are great.

I've made a commitment figure you out.

Where you were made to what you're all about.

Nicaraguan to Dominican it makes no difference.

I just wanna taste every part of your amazing flavors.

At times, I've closed my eyes and been mesmerized.

Releasing the smoke slowly as I listen to various stories.

I chose you today, but sometimes there's a delay.

27

I don't know which one will make my day.

All I know is at the end of it all, I know you'll be my

resolve.

I'm not accepting any calls.

Just going to enjoy my time with you.

Today's choice to smoke the very best.

You know the way to caress my lips just right.

Turn my day from stressed to relaxed and light.

Stogie, stick, cigar you are

By far

One of my greatest pleasures.

SMOKING LOUNGE OF CHOICE

What's your smoking lounge of choice?

Is it where you feel you have a voice.

The place where you can mingle.

Whether your single

Or with a mate

On a date.

Do you prefer laid back and real where you can just chill?

D&B is definitely a thrill.

Lasoa is where I get real comfortable.

The home lounge brings in a crowd.

I spent time in Elite which was a treat.

Cunoma where debonair greets you at the door.

Vinetti's in the back when you wanna climax.

Blowin Smoke when you're really in the mood to sit back
and relax.

The Smoking Jacket is in a different bracket.

Astute Gentlemen where you are sure to make new friends.

The Boardroom is complete with etiquette and style.

What's your smoke of choice?

Do you need assistance in discovering your likes and
dislikes?

You'll get assistance at the door.

It won't be a bore.

At any of these lounges and so many more.

You never know what's in store.

Keep an open mind as you light your cigar.

You are going to a different kind of bar.

Don't be surprised if you meet a movie or sports star.

Cigar lounges bring us together very differently.

I've met some great people consequently.

Forming relationships and friendships that don't reflect
negatively.

We just sit back in Blowin Smoke.

Meet the funniest people in D&B.

Relax, but have fun at Lasoa.

Go in cute, but not aloof at Astute.

And really chill at Cunoma.

The turn up at Vinetti's without the confetti.

Enter with style and grace at the Boardroom.

And I might cap the night with a Betty.

Whose ready?

The Jacket will have you leaving with a cigar stack.

And that's a fact.

DARK IN HERE

It was dark in here.

I wanted to make it clear.

Instead of walking over to the switch, I pulled out my light.

My torch to be exact.

Presented with the facts.

I looked over at my stack.

Delighted at my new shipment.

Knowing that my smoke would hit the ceiling.

This ventilation system is eliminating the smoke.

Allowing me to pull and draw from the finest cigars.

Savoring each moment without any choking.

Which gage do I like?

Well, it depends.

What mood am I in?

If you're a beginner maybe only put the edge of the tip in.

Make sure this is where you begin.

The objective is not to be overwhelmed.

But, where do you stand?

Robusto, Maduro, Corona or Churchill.

Whatever you like let your taste buds devour.

And real smokers blow smoke in the air no matter the hour.

WHEN I TASTED YOU

When I tasted you.

I knew you were the one.

The smoke that circled me told me to savor and show my

love.

Engulfed with the smoke.

I wasn't going to choke

I would just take my time and make you mine.

Pour a glass of wine.

You taste so divine.

Got down to the band.

I start to undress my man.

Admire the way you stand.

And the ash that can withstand.

You burn evenly.

Leaving me wanting more.

This is not a chore.

This time with you is not a bore.

I'm waiting to see what taste are in store.

Tasting you and licking you down to the bare skin.

This is where it begins.

Again and again.

I am your undercover lover.

PUT THE TIP IN

Just put the tip in.

You know what I like.

A bit of a tease before you go deep.

Deeply intoxicating me with your layered flavors.

The way you allow me to inhale every part of you.

You give me permission to swallow.

You prefer to be wet and enjoy my every touch.

If I forget you too long you will need more fire.

The best thing about you is you aren't a liar.

I can expect great things from you.

You soothe me after a long day.

Every now and then I ask you to stay.

Pack you away and you come home with me.

I don't want things to move too fast.

It needs to last.

How amazing this can be in the morning.

I know you are ready when we arise.

Pleased to know you are just as ready as me and that's no

surprise.

NEVER GET ANGRY WITH YOU

I would never get angry with you.

I love your shape, taste and length in my mouth.

How could I be upset with you my Upsetter.

Your taste is like no other.

Each day I'm trying to climb.

Gotta stay focused and do the work as I enjoy my Elevation
to the top.

You are the platinum stick in my mouth.

Perdomo lit bright.

I can see the delay in your burn.

My next stick wants his turn.

Maduro is feeling deprived.

Saw me stroking on you.

Nearly choking on you.

I went too deep.

Must admit you are a keeper.

I'm grateful for your rear my Acid.

As I turn on my tunes and blast it.

TASTE

I love the way you taste in my mouth.

It appears as though you came

Out of nowhere.

You were passed to me.

Gifted to me.

When I lit you up and took a drag.

It felt like you expanded down to my throat.

I almost choked.

I had to revoke

The instinct to...

Quit.

No way was I gonna sit

Back and not learn the value of you.

WHAT CIGAR ARE YOU?

From the wrapper

The binder

The filler too.

What cigar are you?

Lover of the leaf.

What makes it complete?

The appropriate cutter and light will make this a treat.

Take your time and puff slow you have nowhere to go.

You will create the perfect ash.

The one that is suitable to last.

LOVE THE WAY YOU TASTE

I love the way you taste in my mouth

It appears as though you came

Out of nowhere

You were passed to me

Gifted to me.

When I lit you up and took a drag

It felt like you expanded down to my throat I almost

choked

 I had to revoke

The instinct to Quit

No way was I gonna sit back and not learn the value of

you

The benefit of what you have inside

 I'm sticking by your side

Understanding the uniqueness but peacefulness you

provide

You're the perfect passenger and you never meet a

stranger

No matter the season I can smoke you for any reason

Some try to when they're suspected of treason

And there are plenty

Who will try it Blow smoke and screens?

Yes, you know how they pretend to understand you,

but your smoke is relaxing and captivating.

The peace it provides should be no surprise.

TODAY IS THE DAY

Today is the day
I've claimed my stakes.
There is true love in this union and nothing about it is
fake.
I can truly rely on you.
This union is rare.
You leave nothing to spare.
I absolutely love what we share.
When I pull –
You share how much you care.
I'm here for the long haul.
Even if there's a temporary stall.
I'll just light you back up.
And as I await your new flame I'll fill up this cup.

BLOW IN YOUR FACE

The aroma and taste will not go to waste.

I'm convinced that the smoke that is engulfed right here.

Will stay near.

I won't blow the smoke in your face.

Use your etiquette rules.

You may go to any cigar lounge you choose.

Networking and patronizing and making new connections.

No matter your choice.

Ambiance, customer service or the humidor selection.

As you make your determination about what stick you enjoy.

Be open to trying something new.

Despite the few.

Don't be close minded

And easily offended.

It's a good time.

Don't be hesitant about selecting the best.

You have choices and there are many sticks to choose
from.
The humidor at home should full of some.
Enjoy your smoke
Relax, don't choke.
This is a smooth and wind down experience.

TASTED MANY

I've tasted many.

Wanted plenty.

Experienced various sizes and shapes in my mouth.

Often times influenced by your taste and not the cost.

Satisfied at the way you fit perfectly in my mouth.

Although you shrink the longer I hold you.

I'm still enamored and want more.

Fitting day is a dream come true.

The day I get to show you how much I value you.

Showing you off in my traveling humidor.

You are the stick of my choice.

I'm so committed to you.

Can see me spending the rest of my life with you.

But, I better not make any commitments just yet.

This might just be moving too fast.

I'm willing to compromise.

To be honest, let's put it all on the line.

I really want you.

I just want to continue our open relationship.

You're never bothered by the different sticks I may
pick from time to time.
And no matter what.
When I light you up.
You deliver.
Give me everything I need.
And do so with such ease.
By the end of our time.
You've pleased me in every way.
I was able to get you to stay.
Now, I'm going to make a new selection.

AMBIANCE

The ambiance is real

You will want to sit still.

Basking in the stillness you will

Find a seat and begin to relax

Stay on track

And be sure to add tobacco tax

The chill and relaxation provided is pure facts.

I am not an expert, but I can read you this excerpt

Poetic stories of how this lifestyle works

Just be open to networking and approach

You meet people with various background stories

As you all select cigars from the inventory.

As some claim their favorite chair as territory

And others move about the lounge

Various conversations and sounds

Exude within the walls all around.

And although we're not bound.

It is a fun, relaxing and peaceful place.

With each puff you've exhaled the troubles of the day

away.

It is no longer on display.

Revealed by the creases in your face.

It is now dissolved and dissipated to release with ease.

BAZAAR

Do you find it bazaar?

That a cigar

Will keep you where you are

For hours

And although I'm not revealing my superpowers.

I am puffing and parlaying.

There won't be any delaying.

And during these smoke sessions there's no playing

I'm staying.

Right here with you.

Where the cloud of smoke allows me to revoke anything

not meant for me.

Ultimately, who will you be.

Realize the power you hold within.

Don't be scared to just begin.

You'll be pleased when you win.

Some say smoking is a sin.

No way this hobby with friends

Is my downfall.

Whether you decide to stall

And take your time to get to the humidor.

Just make sure you make your way through that door.

Its cigar lounge etiquette.

And, it's as simple as that.

THE WAY I SEE IT

The way I see it

You are brilliant

The feeling you provide is consistent.

Provides me with peace and tranquility and reveals my

resilience.

The thoughts that flow through my mind.

And over time.

I've made you mine.

Although others may smoke one like you

What we have is personal.

I'm able to be versatile.

This is truly a lifestyle.

The culture and experience of smoking a cigar.

Helps to bring out more of my artistic and creative style.

Write until my message is complete.

No matter what happens around me I don't accept defeat.

I just sit back.

Light up and realize I have no lack.

Allowing the smoke to be signs of the days release.

While considering my next life move for gain and increase.

As I nestle in comfortably and hold on to my peace.

READER REVIEWS

**Keya's poems are great advertisements for cigar establishments. She makes it sound like they are all cool places, just a good feeling no matter which one you visit. She gives a good description about smoking cigars. "JT" St. Louis, Missouri*

**Keya writes inspirational poetry aimed at those engaged in the Cigar Lifestyle. This poets message describes how a true cigar smoker feels each time they step into a cigar lounge humidor or choose a stick from their personal stash, cut it, light it and engage in true intimacy with their favorite stick. She shows her true connection and intimacy with something she believes and enjoys. When Keya delivers her poetry verbally it is always delivered with great confidence, expression and passion. She is a grown and sexy poet. "Dave Butler" Dallas, Texas*

**Reading Keya's poetic expressions I immediately felt led to light up my favorite cigar in a comforting and*

53

KEYA S. MCCLAIN

relaxing environment. Her poems immediately draw you in to hat I like to call a climatic cigar experience where you can relax and unwind. "Janell Oliphant" Dallas, Texas

CIGAR CHRONICLES: SISTER OF THE LEAF STORYTELLING

Made in the USA
Monee, IL
28 September 2020